Edith Nesbit

Songs of Love and Empire

Edith Nesbit

Songs of Love and Empire

ISBN/EAN: 9783337007164

Printed in Europe, USA, Canada, Australia, Japan

Cover: Foto ©Thomas Meinert / pixelio.de

More available books at **www.hansebooks.com**

SONGS OF
LOVE AND EMPIRE

By E. NESBIT

AUTHOR OF "LAYS AND LEGENDS," "A POMANDER OF VERSE," ETC

WESTMINSTER
ARCHIBALD CONSTABLE & CO
1898

"AFTER Sixty Years" appeared on June 22, 1897, in the *Daily News*; "To the Queen of England" and many other verses in the *Pall Mall Gazette*; "A Song of Peace and Honour" and "A Song of Trafalgar" in the *Daily Chronicle*, and certain other verses in the *Athenæum*. To the Editors of these papers my thanks are due.

TO HUBERT BLAND

TO you the harvest of my toil has come,
  Because of all that lies its sheaves between;
  You taught me first what Love and Empire mean,
And to your hands I bring my harvest home.

CONTENTS

	PAGE
Absolution	167
Adventurer, The	58
After Sixty Years	11
Appeal, The	93
"At Evening Time there Shall be Light"	150
At the Sound of the Drum	67
Ballad of the White Lady, The	43
Betrayed	109
By Faith with Thanksgiving	91
Chains Invisible	147
Christmas Hymn	164
Crown of Life, The	157
Dirge	125
Discretion	86

CONTENTS

	PAGE
EBB-TIDE	132
ENTREATY	83
EVENING PRAYER	162
EVENING SONG	129
FAITH	62
FAUTE DE MIEUX	99
FEBRUARY	139
FOREST POOL, THE	84
GHOST BEREFT, THE	50
GOOSE GIRL, THE	69
GUARDIAN ANGEL, THE	74
HAUNTED	123
HEART OF GRIEF, THE	115
HEART OF JOY, THE	113
HEART OF SADNESS, THE	111
IN ECLIPSE	103
IN THE ENCHANTED TOWER	60
LAST ACT, THE	97
"LOVE WELL THE HOUR"	107
MAGNIFICAT	159
MAIDENHOOD	152

CONTENTS

	PAGE
MEDWAY SONG	144
MONK, THE	155
NEW COLLEGE GARDENS, OXFORD	135
OFFERING, THE	82
ON THE DOWNS	133
OUT OF HOPE	121
PEDLAR, THE	71
PORTRAIT, A	80
PRELUDE	66
PROMISE OF SPRING, THE	141
QUEEN OF ENGLAND, THE	3
REFUSAL, THE	64
REQUIEM	117
"SHEPHERDS ALL AND MAIDENS FAIR"	77
SONG IN AUTUMN	95
SONG OF LONG AGO	101
SONG OF PEACE AND HONOUR	35
SONG OF TRAFALGAR	26
SPECIAL PLEADING	105
SPRING SONG	88
TEINT NEUTRE	119

CONTENTS

	PAGE
"This Desirable Mansion"	131
To a Tulip Bulb	137
Too Late	90
Trafalgar Day	24
Vain Spell, The	55
Waterloo Day	32

I

L.E.

I

B

TO THE QUEEN OF ENGLAND

[JUNE 22, 1897]

COME forth! the world's aflame with flags and
    flowers,
  The shout of bells fills full the shattered air,
This is the crown of all your golden hours,
    More than all other hours august and fair;
      This did the years prepare,
A triumph for our Lady and our Queen,
More rich than any king in any land hath seen.

TO THE QUEEN

Clothed are your streets with scarlet, gold, and blue,
Flowers under foot and banners over head,
And while your people's voice storms Heaven for you
About your way are voiceless blessings shed,
And over you are spread
Wide wings of love, free love, tamed to your hand,
Love that gold cannot buy, nor Majesty command.

Not these mere visible millions only, share
Your triumph—here all English hearts beat high,
Nations far off your royal colours wear,
And swell with unheard voice this loyal cry
That strikes the English sky:
A cloud of unseen witnesses is here
To testify how great is England's Queen, and dear.

OF ENGLAND

From out the grey-veiled past, long years away,
    Come visionary faces, vision-led,
And splendid shapes that are not of our day,
    The spirits of the mute and mighty dead,
        To see how Time has sped
The fortunes of their England, and behold
How much more great she is than in the days
    of old.

The world can see them not; but you can see—
    You the inheritor of all the past
Wherein the dead, in noble heraldry,
    Blazoned the shield of England, and forecast
        The charge it bears at last—
More splendid than the azure and the or
Of the French lilies lost—long lost and sorrowed
    for.

TO THE QUEEN

Here be the weaponed men, the English folk,
    Who in long ships across the swan's bath fared,
In whose rude tongue the voice of Freedom spoke,
    In whose rough hands the sword was bright and bared—
    The men who did and dared,
And to their sons bequeathed the fighting blood
That drives to Victory and will not be withstood.

Here, in your ordered festival, O Queen,
    Mixed with the crowd and all unseen of these,
On their long swords the wild Norse rovers lean
    And watch the progress of your pageantries,
    And on this young June breeze
Float the bright pennons of the Cressy spears—
Shine shadowy shafts that fell, as snow falls, at Poitiers.

OF ENGLAND

Here flutter phantom flags that once flew free
    Above the travail of the tournament;
Here gleam old swords, once wet for Liberty;
    Old blood-stiff banners, worn with war and rent,
    Are with your fresh flowers blent,
And by your crown, where love and fame consort,
Shines the unvanquished cloven crown of Agincourt.

Upon your river where, by day and night,
    Your world-adventuring ships come home again,
Glide ghostly galleons, manned by men of might
    Who plucked the wings and singed the beard of Spain;
    The men who, not in vain,
Saved to the children of a world new-trod
The birth-tongue of our land, her freedom, and her God.

TO THE QUEEN

Princes who lived to make our England great,
    Poets who wreathed her greatness with their song,
Wise men who steered her heavy ship of State,
    Brave men who steered her battle-ships along,
        In spectral concourse throng
To applaud the consummated power and pride
Of that belovèd land for which they lived and died.

The thousand un-named heroes who, sword-strong,
    Ploughed the long acre wherein Empire grows
Wide as the world, and long as Time is long—
    These mark the crescence of the English rose
        Whose thorny splendour glows
O'er far-off subject lands, by alien waves,
A crown for England's brow, a garland for her graves.

OF ENGLAND

And faces out of unforgotten years,
    Faces long hidden by death's misty screen,
Faces you still can scarcely see for tears,
    Will smile on you to-day and near you lean,
        O Mother, Wife, and Queen!
With whispered love too sacred and too dear
For any ear than yours, Mother and Wife, to hear.

Lady, the crowd will vaunt to-day your fame,
    Daughter and heir of many mighty kings,
The Queen of England, whose imperial name
    From England's heart and lips tumultuous springs
        In prayers and thanksgivings,
Because your greatness and her greatness shine
Merged each in each, as stars their beams that intertwine.

TO THE QUEEN OF ENGLAND

Yet in the inmost heart, where folded close
    The richest treasures of the poorest lie,
Love, whose clear eyes see many secrets, knows
    A nobler name than Queen to call you by,
        And breathes it silently ;
But, 'mid His listening crowd of angels, One
Shall speak your name and say, "Faithful and good, well done!"

AFTER SIXTY YEARS

RING, bells! flags, fly! and let the great crowd
    roar
  Its ecstasy. Let the hid heart in prayer
Lift up your name. God bless you evermore,
    Lady, who have the noblest crown to wear
        That ever woman wore.
A jewel, in the front of time, shall blaze
    This day, of all your days commemorate;
    With Time's white bays your brows are laureate,
And England's love shall garland all your days.

    *   *   *   *

AFTER SIXTY YEARS

When England's crown, to Love's acclaim, was laid
   On the soft brightness of a maiden's hair,
Amid delight, Love trembled, half afraid,
     To give that little head such weight to bear,—
        Bind on so slight a maid
A kingdom's purple—bid her hands hold high
   The sceptre and the heavy orb of power,
   To give to youth and beauty for a dower
Care and a crown, sorrow and sovereignty.

But from our hearts sprang an intenser flame
   When loyal Love met tender Love half way,
And, in love's script, wrote on the scroll of fame,
   Entwined with all the splendour of that day,
       The letters of her name.
Then as fair roses grow 'mid leaves of green,
   Love amid loyalty grew strong and close,
   To hedge a pleasaunce round our Royal rose,
Our sovereign maiden flower, our child, our Queen.

AFTER SIXTY YEARS

The trumpets spake—in sonorous triumph shout,
  Their speech found echo in the hundred guns;
From countless towers the answering bells rang out,
  And England's heart spoke clamorous, through her sons,
    The exulting land throughout.
Down streets ablaze with light the flags unfurled,
  Along dark, lonely hills the joy-fires crept,
  And eager swords within their scabbards leapt
To guard our Lady and Queen against the world.

Those swords are rusted now. Good men and true
  Dust in the dust are laid who held her dear;
But from their grave the bright flower springs anew,
  Which for her festival we bring her here,
    The long years' meed and due;

AFTER SIXTY YEARS

The bud of homage graffed on chivalry.
   God took the souls that shrined the jewel of love,
   But made their sons inheritors thereof,
In endless gold entail of loyalty.

Time, compensating life, the fruit bestowed
   When in spent perfume passed the flower of youth;
Her feet were set upon the upward road,
   Her face was turned towards the star of truth
      That in her soul abode.
With youth the maid's bright brow was garlanded
   But richer crowns adorn the dear white hair;
   The gathered love of all the years lies there,
In coronal benediction on her head.

AFTER SIXTY YEARS

She is of our blood, for hath not she, too, met
    The angels of delight and of despair?
Does not she, too, remember and forget
    How bitter or how bright the lost days were?
        Her eyes have tears made wet;
She has seen joy unveilèd even as we,
    Has laid upon cold clay the heart-warm kiss,
    She has known Sorrow for the king he is;
She has held little children on her knee.

Mother, dear Mother, these your children rise
    And call you blessèd, and shall we not, too,
Who are your children in the greater wise,
    And love you for our land and her for you?
        The blessing sanctifies
Your children as they breathe it at your knees,
    And, bringing little gifts from very far,
    Where the great nurseries of your Empire are,
Your children's blessings throng from over seas.

AFTER SIXTY YEARS

On Love's spread wings, and over leagues of space,
  Homage is borne from far-off sun-steeped lands ;
From many a domed mysterious Eastern place,
  Where Secresy holds Time between her hands,
    The children of your race
Reach English hands towards your English throne ;
  And from the far South turn blue English eyes,
That never saw the blue of English skies,
Yet call you Mother, and your land their own.

Where 'mid great trees the mighty waters flow
  In arrogant submission to your sway,
In fur of price your northern hunters go,
  And shafts of ardent greeting fly your way
    Across the splendid snow ;

AFTER SIXTY YEARS

And isles that with their coral, safe and small,
   Rock in the cradle of the tropic seas,
   In soft, strange speech join in the litanies
That pride and prayer breathe at your festivsl.

All round the world, on every far-off sea,
   In wind-ploughed oceans and in sun-kissed bays,
By every busy wharf and chattering quay,
   Some cantle of your Empire sails or stays—
      Flaunts your supremacy
Against the winds of all the world, and flies
   Your flag triumphant between blue and blue,
   Blazons to sun and star the name of you,
And spreads your glory between seas and skies.

There is no cottage garden, sunny-sweet,
   There is no pasture where our shepherds tend
Their quiet flocks, no red-roofed village street,
   But holds for you the love-wish of a friend,
      Blent with high homage meet;

AFTER SIXTY YEARS

No little farm among the cornfields lone,
　　No little cot upon the uplands bare,
　　But hears to-day in blessing and in prayer
One name, Victoria, and that name your own.

From the vast cities where the giant's might,
　　Pauseless, resistless, moves by night and day,
From hidden mines where day is one with night,
　　From weary lives whose days and nights are grey
　　　　And empty of delight,
From lives that rhyme to sunshine and the spring,
　　From happiness at flood and hope at ebb,
　　Rose the magnificent and mingled web
That floats, your banner, at your thanksgiving.

Throned on the surety of a splendid past,
　　With present glory clothed as with the sun,

AFTER SIXTY YEARS

Crowned with the future's hopes, you know at last
What treasure from the years your life has won ; .
Behold, your hands hold fast
The moon of Empire, and its sway controls
The tides of war and peace, while in those hands
Lies tender homage out of all the lands
Against whose feet your furthest ocean rolls.

How seems your life, looked back at through the years ?
Much love, much sorrow, dead desires, lost dreams,
A great life lived out greatly ; hidden tears,
And smiles for daily wear ; strong plans and schemes,
And mighty hopes and fears ;

AFTER SIXTY YEARS

War in the South and murder in the East,
  And England's heart-throbs echoed by your heart
  When loss, and labour, and sorrow were her part,
Or when Fate bade her to some flower-crowned feast.

Red battle-fields whereon your soldiers died,
  Green pastoral fields saved by the blood of these,
Duty that bade mere sorrow stand aside,
  And love transforming anguish into ease;
    Long longing satisfied,
Great secrets wrenched from Nature's grudging breast,
  The fruit of knowledge plucked for all to eat,—
  These have you known, Life's circle is complete,
And, knowing these, you know what is Life's best:

AFTER SIXTY YEARS

The dear small secrets of our common life,
  The English woods and hills, the English home,
The common joys and griefs of Mother and wife,
  Joy coming, going—griefs that go and come,
    Soul's peace amid world's strife ;
Hours when the Queen's cares leave the woman free ;
  Dear friendships, where the friend forgets the Queen
And stoops to wear a dearer, homelier mien,
And be more loved than mere Queens rise to be.

And, in your hour of triumph, when you shine
  The centre of our triumph's blazing star,
And, gazing down your long life's lustrous line,
  Behold how great your life-long glories are,
    Yet, in your heart's veiled shrine,

AFTER SIXTY YEARS

No splendour of all splendours that have been
   Will brim your eyes with tremulous thanks-
      givings,
   But little memories of little things—
The treasures of the woman, not the Queen.

Yet, Queen, because the love of you hath wound
   A golden girdle all about the earth,
Because your name is as a trumpet sound
   To call toward you men of English birth
      From the world's outmost bound,
Because old kinsmen, long estranged from home,
   Come, with old foes, to greet you, friend and
      kin,
With kindly eyes behold your guests come in,
See from afar the long procession come!

No Emperor in Rome's Imperial days
   Knew ever such a triumph day as this,

AFTER SIXTY YEARS

Though captive kings bore chains along his ways,
  Though tribute from the furthest isles was his,
      With pageant and with praise.
For you—free kings and free republics grace
  Your triumph, and across the conquered waves
  Come gifts from friends, not tributes wrung from slaves,
And praise kneels, clothed in love, before your face.

Ring, bells! flags, fly! and let the great crowd roar
  Its ecstasy! Let the hid heart in prayer
Lift up your name! God bless you evermore,
  Lady, who have the noblest crown to wear
      That ever monarch wore.
For, 'mid this day's triumphal voluntaries,
  Your name shines like the splendour of the sun,
  Because your name with England's name is one,
As Hers, thank God! is one with Liberty's.

TRAFALGAR DAY

LAURELS, bring laurels, sheaves on sheaves,
Till England's boughs are bare of leaves !
    Soon comes the flower more rare, more dear
Than any laurel this year weaves—
    The Aloe of the hundredth year
        Since from the smoke of Trafalgar
    He passed to where the heroes are,
Nelson, who passed and yet is here,
    Whose dust is fire beneath our feet,
    Whose memory mans our fleet.

TRAFALGAR DAY

Laurels, bring laurels, since they hold
His England's tears in each green fold,
   His England's joy, his England's pride,
His England's glories manifold.
   Yet what was Victory since he died?
     And what was Death since he lives yet,
     Above a Nation's worship set,
   Above her heroes glorified?—
     Nelson, who made our flag a star
     To lead where Victories are!

A SONG OF TRAFALGAR

LIKE an angry sun, like a splendid star,
    War gleams down the long years' track;
They strain at the leash, the dogs of war,
    And who shall hold them back?
"Let loose the pack: we are English bred,
    We will meet them full and fair
With the flag of England over our head,
    And his hand to keep it there!"

A SONG OF TRAFALGAR

So spake our fathers. Our flag, unfurled,
    Blew brave to the north and south ;
An iron answer we gave the world,
    For we spoke by the cannon's mouth.
But he who taught us the word to say
    Grew dumb as his Victory sang,
And England mourned on her triumph day,
    And wept while her joy-bells rang.

Long hour by hour, and long day by day,
    The swift years crept apace,
The patient, the coral-insect way,
    To cover the dear dead face.
O foolish rabble of envious years,
    Who wist not the dead must rise,
His name is music still in our ears,
    His face a light to our eyes !

A SONG OF TRAFALGAR

Bring hither your laurels, the fading sign
    Of a deathless love and pride ;
These cling more close than the laurels twine,
    They are strong as the world is wide :
At the feet of Virtue in Valour clad
    Shall glory and love be laid,
While Glory sings to an English lad,
    Or Love to an English maid.

Wherever the gleams of an English fire
    On an English roof-tree shine,
Wherever the fire of a youth's desire
    Is laid upon Honour's shrine,
Wherever brave deeds are treasured and told,
    In the tale of the deeds of yore
Like jewels of price in a chain of gold
    Are the name and the fame he bore.

A SONG OF TRAFALGAR

Wherever the track of our English ships
    Lies white on the ocean foam,
His name is sweet to our English lips
    As the names of the flowers at home;
Wherever the heart of an English boy
    Grows big with a deed of worth,
Such names as his name have begot the same,
    Such hearts will bring it to birth.

They say that his England, grown tired and old,
    Lies drunk by her heavy hoard;
They say her hands have the grasp of the gold
    But not the grip of the sword,
That her robe of glory is rent and shred,
    And that winds of shame blow through:
Speak for your England, O mighty Dead,
    In the deeds you would have her do!

A SONG OF TRAFALGAR

Small skill have we to fight with the pen
    Who fought with the sword of old,
For the sword that is wielded of Englishmen
    Is as much as one hand can hold.
Yet the pen and the tongue are safe to use,
    And the coward and the wise choose these;
But fools and brave were our English crews
    When Nelson swept the seas.

'Tis the way of a statesman to fear and fret,
    To ponder and pause and plan,
But the way of Nelson was better yet,
    For that was the way of a man;
They would teach us smoothness, who once were
    rough,
    They have bidden us palter and pray,
But the way of Nelson was good enough,
    For that was the fighting way.

A SONG OF TRAFALGAR

If Nelson's England must stoop to bear
    What never honour should brook,
In vain does the tomb of her hero wear
    The laurel his brow forsook;
In vain was the speech from the lips of her guns,
    If now must her lips refrain;
In vain has she made us, her living sons,
    Her dead have made her in vain.

So here with your bays be the dear head crowned,
    Lay flowers where the dear dust lies,
And wreathe his column with laurel round
    To point his fame to the skies;
But the greenest laurel that ever grew
    Is the laurel that's yet to win;
Crowned with his laurels he waits for You
    To bring Your laurels in!

WATERLOO DAY

[June 18]

THIS is the day of our glory; this is our day to weep.
Under her dusty laurels England stirs in her sleep;
Dreams of her days of honour, terrible days that are dead,
Days of the making of story, days when the sword was red,

When all her fate and her future hung on the naked blade,
When by the sword of her children her place in the world was made,

WATERLOO DAY

When Honour sounded the trumpet and Valour leapt to obey,
And Heroes bought us the Empire that statesmen would sell to-day.

England, wanton and weary, sunk in a slothful ease,
Has slain in her wars her thousands, but her tens of thousands in peace:
And the cowards grieve for her glory; their glory is in their shame;
They are glad of the moth in her banners, and the rust on her shining name.

Oh, if the gods would send us a balm for our sick, sad years,
Let them send us a sight of the scarlet, and the sound of the guns in our ears!

WATERLOO DAY

For valour and faith and honour—these grow where the red flower grows,
And the leaves for the Nation's healing must spring from the blood of her foes.

A SONG OF PEACE AND HONOUR
[DECEMBER, 1895]
TO THE QUEEN

LADY and Queen, for whom our laurels twine,
   Upon whose head the glories of our land
      In one immortal diadem are met,
   Embodied England, in whose woman-hand
      The sceptre of Imperial sway is set,
      Receive this song of mine!
For you are England, and her bays grow green
   To deck your brow, your goodness lends her grace,
   And in our hearts your face is as Her face;
The Mother-Country is the Mother-Queen.

   *   *   *   *   *

We, men of England, children of her might,
   With all our Mother's record-roll of glory,
      Great with her greatness, noble by her name,

A SONG OF PEACE AND HONOUR

Drank with our mothers' milk our Mother's story,
And in our veins the splendour of her fame
Made strong our blood and bright;
And to her absent sons her name has been
Familiar music heard in distant lands,
Heart of our heart and sinews of our hands,
England, our Mother, our Mistress and our Queen!

Out of the thunderous echoes of the past
Through the gold-dust of centuries we hear
Her voice, "O children of a royal line,
Sons of her heart, whom England holdeth dear,
Mine was the Past—make ye the future mine
All glorious to the last!"
And, as we hear her, cowards grow to men,
And men to heroes, and the voice of fear
Is as a whisper in a deaf man's ear,
And the dead past is quick in us again.

A SONG OF PEACE AND HONOUR

Her robe is woven of glory and renown,
   Hers are the golden-laden Argosies,
     And lordship of the wild and watery ways,
   Her flag is blown across the utmost seas:
     Dead nations built her throne, and kingdoms blaze
       For jewels in her crown.
Her Empire like a girdle doth enfold
   The world; her feet upon her foes are set;
   She wears the steel-wrought, blood-bright amulet
Won by her children in the days of old.

Yet in a treasury of such gems as these
   Which power and sovereignty and kingship fill
     To the vast limit of the circling sun,
   England, our Mother, in her heart holds still,
     As her most precious jewel, save only one,
       The priceless pearl of peace—

A SONG OF PEACE AND HONOUR

Peace plucked from out the very heart of war
 Through the long agony of strenuous years,
 Made pure by blood and sanctified by tears,
A pearl to lie where England's treasures are.

O peaceful English lanes all white with may,
 O English meadows where the grass grows tall,
  O red-roofed village, field and farm and fold
 Where the long shadows of the elm-trees fall
  On the wide pastures which the sun calls gold
  And twilit dew calls gray ;—
These are the home, the happy cradle-place
 Of every man who has our English tongue,
 Sprung from those loins from which our sires have sprung,
Heirs of the glory of our mighty race!

A SONG OF PEACE AND HONOUR

Brothers, we hold the pearl of priceless worth:
   Shall Peace, our pearl, by us be cast aside?
      Is it not more to us than all things are?
   Nay, Peace is precious as the world is wide,
      But England's honour is more precious far
         Than all the heavens and earth.
Were honour outcast from her supreme place
   Our pearl of Peace no more a pearl would shine,
But, trampled under-foot of cowards and swine,
Rot in the mire of a deserved disgrace.

Know then, O ye our brothers over sea,
   We will not cast our pearl of Peace away,
      But, holding it, we wait; and if, at last,
   The whole world came against us in array,
      If all our glory into darkness passed,
         Our Empire ceased to be,

A SONG OF PEACE AND HONOUR

Yet should we still have chosen the better part
  Though in the dust our kingdoms were cast down,
  Though lost were every jewel in our crown
We still should wear our jewel in our heart.

So, for our Mother's honour, if it must
  Let Peace be lost, but lost the worthier way;
    Not trampled down, but given, for her sake
  Who forged of many an iron yesterday
    The golden song that gold-tongued fame shall wake
      When we are dust, in dust:
For brotherhood and strife and praise and blame
  And all the world, even to our very land,
    Weighed in the balance, are as a grain of sand
Against the honour of our English name!

II

THE BALLAD OF THE WHITE LADY

SIR GEOFFREY met the white lady
  Upon his marriage morn,
Her eyes were blue as cornflowers are,
  Her hair was gold like corn.

Sir Geoffrey gave the white lady
  A posy of roses seven,
"You are the fairest May," said he,
  "That ever strayed from Heaven."

THE BALLAD OF

Sir Geoffrey by the white lady
   Was lured away to shame,
For seven long years of prayers and tears
   No tidings of him came.

Then she who should have been his bride
   A mighty oath she swore,
" For seven long years I have wept and prayed,
   Now I will pray no more.

"Since God and all the saints of Heaven
   Bring not my lord to me,
I will go down myself to hell
   And bring him back," said she.

    *   *   *   *   *

She crept to the white lady's bower,
   The taper's flame was dim,
And there Sir Geoffrey lay asleep,
   And the white witch sat by him.

THE WHITE LADY

Her arm was laid across his neck,
   Her gold hair on his face,
And there was silence in the room
   As in a burial-place.

And there were gems and carven cups,
   And 'broidered bridal gear—
"Whose bridal is this?" the lady said,
   "And what knight have ye here?"

"The good knight here ye know full well,
   He was your lord, I trow,
But I have taken him from your side,
   And I am his lady now.

"This seven year with right good cheer
   We twain our bridal keep,
So take for your mate another knight
   And let my dear lord sleep."

THE BALLAD OF

Then up and spake Sir Geoffrey's bride,
  "What bridal cheer is this?
I would think scorn to have the lips
  Who could not have the kiss!

" I would think scorn to take the half
  Who could not have the whole;
I would think scorn to steal the body
  Who could not take the soul!

"For, though ye hold his body fast
  This seven weary year,
His soul walks ever at my side
  And whispers in my ear.

" I would think scorn to hold in sleep
  What, if it waked, would flee,
So let his body join his soul
  And both fare forth with me;

THE WHITE LADY

"For I have learned a spell more strong
  Than yours that laid him low,
And I will speak it for his sake
  Because I love him so!"

The white lady threw back her hair,
  Her eyes began to shine—
"His soul is thine these seven years?—
  To-night it shall be mine!

"I have been brave to hold him here
  While seven long years befell,
Rather than let a bridal be
  Whose seed should flower in hell.

"I have not looked into his eyes
  Nor joined my lips to his,
For fear his soul should spring to flame
  And shrivel at my kiss.

THE BALLAD OF

"I have been brave to watch his sleep
   While the long hours come and go,
To hold the body without the soul,
   Because I love him so.

"But since his soul this seven year
   Has sat by thee," she said,
"His body and soul to-night shall lie
   Upon my golden bed.

"Thou hast no need to speak the spell
   That thou hast learned," said she,
"For I will wake him from his sleep
   And take his soul from thee."

She stooped above him where he lay,
   She laid her lips on his;
He stirred, he spake: "These seven long years
   I have waited for thy kiss.

THE WHITE LADY

" My soul has hung upon thy lips
   And trembled at thy breath,
Thou hast given me life in a cup to drink,
   As God will give me death.

" Why didst thou fear to kill my soul
   Which only lives for thee?
Thou hast put seven wasted years,
   O love, 'twixt thee and me."

THE GHOST BEREFT

THE poor ghost came through the wind and rain
And passed down the old dear road again.

Thin cowered the hedges, the tall trees swayed
Like little children that shrank afraid.

The wind was wild and the night was late
When the poor ghost came to the garden gate;

Dank were the flower-beds, heavy and wet,
The weeds stood up where the rose was set.

The wind was angry, the rain beat sore
When the poor ghost came to its own house-door.

THE GHOST BEREFT

"And shall I find her a-weeping still
To think how alone I lie and chill?

"Or shall I find her happy and warm
With her dear head laid on a new love's arm?

"Or shall I find she has learned to pine
For another's love, and not for mine?

"Whatever chance, I have this to my store,
She is mine, my own, for evermore!"

So the poor ghost came through the wind and rain
Till it reached the square bright window pane.

"Oh! what is here in the room so bright?
Roses and love, and a hid delight?

"What lurks in the silence that fills the room?
A cypress wreath from a dead man's tomb?

THE GHOST BEREFT

" What sleeps? What wakes? And oh! can it be
Her heart that is breaking—and not for me?"

Then the poor ghost looked through the window pane,
Though all the glass was wrinkled with rain.

" Oh, there is light, at the feet and head
Twelve tall tapers about the bed.

" Oh, there are flowers, white flowers and rare,
But not the garland a bride may wear.

" Jasmine white and a white white rose,
But its scent is gone where the lost dream goes.

" Straight lilies laid on the strait white bier—
But the room is empty—she is not here!

" Her body lies here, deserted, cold;
And the body that loved it creeps in the mould.

THE GHOST BEREFT

"Was there ever an hour when my Love, set free,
Would not have hastened and come to me?

"Can the soul that loved mine long ago
Be hence and away, and I not know?

"Oh, then God's judgment is on me sore,
For I have lost her for evermore!"

And the poor ghost fared through the wind and rain
To its own appointed place again.

* * * * *

But up in Heaven, where memories cease
Because the blessed have won to peace,

One pale saint shivered, and closer wound
The shining raiment that wrapped her round.

THE GHOST BEREFT

"Oh, fair is Heaven, and glad am I,
Yet I fain would remember the days gone by.

"The past is veiled, and I may not know,
But I think there was sorrow, long ago;

"The sun of Heaven is warm and bright,
But I think there is rain on the earth to-night.

"O Christ, because of Thine own sore pain
Help all poor souls in the wind and rain."

THE VAIN SPELL

THE house sleeps dark and the moon wakes white,
  The fields are alight with dew;
"Oh, will you not come to me, Love, to-night?
  I have waited the whole night through,
                         For I knew,
O Heart of my heart, I knew by my heart,
  That the night of all nights is this,
When elm shall crack and lead shall part,
When moulds shall sunder and shot bolts start
  To let you through to my kiss."

THE VAIN SPELL

So spake she alone in the lonely house.
    She had wrapped her round with the spell,
She called the call, she vowed the vow,
    And the heart she had pledged knew well
That this was the night, the only night,
    When the moulds might be wrenched apart,
When the living and dead, in the dead of the night,
Might clasp once more, in the grave's despite,
    For the price of a living heart.

But out in the grave the corpse lay white
    And the grave clothes were wet with dew;
"Oh, will you not come to me, Love, to-night,
    I have waited the whole night through,
                  For I knew
That I dared not leave my grave for an hour
    Since the hour of all hours is near,

THE VAIN SPELL

When you shall come to the hollow bower,
In a cast of the wind, in a waft of the Power,
  To the heart that to-night beats here!"

The moon grows pale and the house sleeps still;
  Ah, God! do the dead forget?
The grave is white and the bed is chill,
  But a guest may be coming yet.
But the hour has come and the hour has gone
  That never will come again;
Love's only chance is over and done,
And the quick and the dead are twain, not one,
  And the price has been paid in vain.

THE ADVENTURER

THE land of gold was far away,
   The sea a challenge roared between;
   I left my throne, my crown, my queen,
And sailed out of the quiet bay.

I met the challenge of the wave,
   The curses of the winds I mocked:
   The conquered wave my galley rocked,
The wind became my envious slave.

I brought much treasure from afar,
   Spices, and shells, and rich attire;
   Red rubies, fed with living fire,
To lie where all my longings are.

THE ADVENTURER

Heavy with spoil my keel ploughed low
   As slow we sailed into the bay,
   And long ago seemed yesterday
And yesterday looked long ago.

I came in triumph from the sea;
   Bent was my crown, my courts grown mean,
   And on my throne a faded queen
Raised alien eyes, and looked at me.

"My queen! These rubies let me lay
   Upon thy heart, as once my head . . ."
   She smiled pale scorn: "My heart!" she said,
And turned her weary eyes away.

IN THE ENCHANTED TOWER

THE waves in thunderous menace break
　Upon the rocks below my tower,
　And none will dare the Sea-king's power
And venture shipwreck for my sake.

Yet once,—my lamp a path of light
　Across the darkling sea had cast—
　I saw a sail; at last, at last,
It came towards me through the night.

My lamp had been the beacon set
　To lead the ship through mist and foam,
　The ship that came to take me home,
To that far land I half forget.

IN THE ENCHANTED TOWER

But since my tower is built so high,
   And surf-robed rocks curl hid below,
   I quenched my lamp—and, weeping low
I saw my ship go safely by!

FAITH

THROUGH the long night, the deathlong night,
   Along the dark and haunted way,
I knew your hidden face was bright—
   More bright than any day.

And when the faint, insistent moan
   Rose from some weed-grown wayside grave,
I said, "I do not walk alone;
   'Tis easy to be brave."

I never turned to speak with you,
   For all the way was dark and long,
But all the shadows' menace through
   Your silence was my song.

FAITH

I never sought to take your hand,
   For all the way was long and rough;
I taught my soul to understand
   That love was strength enough.

Then, suddenly, the ghosts drew near,
   A ghastly, gliding, tomb-white band;
I called aloud for you to hear,
   My hand besought your hand.

No voice, no touch—the thin ghosts glide
   Where in my dream I dreamed you were—
Night, night, you are not by my side,
   You never have been there!

THE REFUSAL

MINE is a palace fair to see,
   All hung with gold and silver things,
   It is more glorious than a king's,
And crownèd queens might envy me.

Ah, no, I will not let you in!
   Stay rather at the gates and weep
   For all the splendour that I keep,
The treasures that you cannot win.

While you desire and I refuse,
   For both the palace still is here—
   Its turrets gold, its silver gear
Are yours to wish for—mine to use.

THE REFUSAL

But if I let you in, I know
    The spell would break, the palace fade,
    And we stand, trembling and afraid,
Lost in the dark where chill winds blow.

PRELUDE

OUT of the west when the sun was dying
Clouds of white wings came flying, flying,
Wheeling and whirling they swept away
Into the heart of the eastern gray;
But one white dove came straight to my breast
    Out of the west.

Into the west when the dawn was pearly
Clouds of white wings went, dewy-early,
Straight from the world of the waning stars;
O beating pinions! O prison bars!
My dove flies free no more with the rest
    Into the west.

AT THE SOUND OF THE DRUM

ARE you going for a soldier with your curly
   yellow hair,
And a scarlet coat instead of the smock you
   used to wear?
Are you going to drive the foe as you used to
   drive the plough?
   Are you going for a soldier now?

I am going for a soldier, and my tunic is of red
And I'm tired of woman's chatter, and I'll hear
   the drum instead;
I will break the fighting line as you broke your
   plighted vow,
   For I'm going for a soldier now.

AT THE SOUND OF THE DRUM

For a soldier, for a soldier are you sure that you will go,
To hear the drums a-beating and to hear the bugles blow?
I'll make you sweeter music, for I'll swear another vow—
    Are you going for a soldier now?

I am going for a soldier if you'd twenty vows to make;
You must get another sweetheart, with another heart to break,
For I'm sick of lies and women and the harrow and the plough,
    And I'm going for a soldier now!

THE GOOSE-GIRL

I WANDERED lonely by the sea,
   As is my daily use,
I saw her drive across the lea
   The gander and the goose.
The gander and the gray, gray goose,
   She drove them all together;
Her cheeks were rose, her gold hair loose,
   All in the wild gray weather.

"O dainty maid who drive the geese
   Across the common wide,
Turn, turn your pretty back on these
   And come and be my bride.

THE GOOSE-GIRL

I am a poet from the town,
    And, 'mid the ladies there,
There is not one would wear a crown
    With half your charming air!"

She laughed, she shook her pretty head.
    " I want no poet's hand ;
Go read your fairy-books," she said,
    "For this is fairy-land.
My Prince comes riding o'er the leas ;
    He fitly comes to woo,
For I'm a Princess, and my geese
    Were poets, once, like you!"

THE PEDLAR

FLY, fly, my pretty pigeon, fly!
    And see if you can find him;
He has blue eyes—you'll know him by,—
    He wears a pack behind him.
He's gone away—ah! many a mile
    Because he could not please me,
And, oh! 'twill be a weary while
    Ere next he comes to tease me.

He carries wares of every kind,
    Fine ribbons, silks, and laces,
Bargains to rhyme with every mind,
    And hues to suit all faces.

THE PEDLAR

He has gold rings and pretty things
   That other maids will throng for,
Ah, pigeon! spread your pretty wings,
   And fly to him I long for.

Tell him to turn and come again,
   For once I sent him packing;
He offered me a bargain then,
   But wit and price were lacking.
I have the price he asked of me,
   The wit that will not weigh it;
Ah! bid him come again and see
   How gladly I will pay it.

A heart of gold he offered me
   As 'twere a penny fairing,
And only asked a worthless fee,
   This heavy heart I'm wearing.

THE PEDLAR

I would not then—now long and drear
    The white way winds behind him;
Ah! seek him, seek him, Pigeon dear,
    But you will never find him!

THE GUARDIAN ANGEL

WHEN my good-nights and prayers are said
And I am safe tucked up in bed,
I know my guardian angel stands
And holds my soul between his hands.

I cannot see his wings of light
Because I keep my eyes shut tight,
For, if I open them, I know
My pretty angel has to go.

But through the darkness I can hear
His white wings rustling very near;
I know it is his darling wings,
Not Mother folding up my things!

III

"SHEPHERDS ALL AND MAIDENS FAIR"

PIPE, shepherds, pipe, the summer's ripe;
  So wreathe your crooks with flowers;
The world's in tune to Love and June,
  The days are rich in hours,
In rosy hours, in golden hours—
  Love's crown and fortune fair,
So gather gold for Love to hold,
  And flowers for Love to wear!

"SHEPHERDS ALL AND

Sing, maidens, sing! A dancing ring
  Of pleasures speed your way;
Too harsh and dry is fierce July,
  Too maiden-meek was May;
But Love and June their old sweet tune
  Are singing at your ear:
So learn the song and troop along
  To meet your shepherds dear!

Oh, Chloris fair, a rose to wear,
  And gold to spend have I—
When all are gay on this June day
  You would not bid me sigh?
You would not scorn a swain forlorn—
  Each shepherd far and near
Hastes to his sweet, with flying feet,
  As I towards my dear.

MAIDENS FAIR"

No maids there be in Arcady
  But have their shepherds true ;
Must you alone despise the one
  Who only pipes for you ?
You have no ear my pipe to hear
  Though all for you it be ;
And I no eyes for her who sighs
  And only sings for me !

A PORTRAIT

LIKE the sway of the silver birch in the breeze
of dawn
    Is her dainty way;
Like the gray of a twilight sky or a starlit lawn
    Are her eyes of gray;
Like the clouds in their moving white
    Is her breast's soft stir;
And white as the moon and bright
    Is the soul of her.

Like murmur of woods in spring ere the leaves
be green,
    Like the voice of a bird

A PORTRAIT

That sings by a stream that sings through the
    night unseen,
        So her voice is heard.
And the secret her eyes withhold
        In my soul abides,
For white as the moon and cold
        Is the heart she hides.

THE OFFERING

WHAT will you give me for this heart of mine,
  No heart of gold—and yet my dearest treasure?
It has its graces—it can ache and pine,
    And beat true time to your sweet voice's measure;
  It bears your name, it lives but for your pleasure:
    What will you give me for this heart I bring,
    That holds my life, my joy, my everything?

How can I ask a price, when all my prayer
  Is that, without return, you will but take it—
Feed it with hope, or starve it to despair,
    Keep it to play with, mock it, crush it, break it,
  And, if your will lies there, at last forsake it?
    Its epitaph shall voice its deathless pride:
    "She held me in her hands until I died."

ENTREATY

O LOVE, let us part now!
Ours is the tremulous, low-spoken vow,
Ours is the spell of meeting hands and eyes.
   The first, involuntary, sacred kiss
Still on our lips in benediction lies.
O Love, be wise!
   Love at its best is worth no more than this—
           Let us part now!

O Love, let us part now!
Ere yet the roses wither on my brow,
Ere yet the lilies wither in your breast,
   Ere the implacable hour shall flower to bear
The seeds of deathless anguish and unrest.
To part is best.
   Between us still the drawn sword flameth fair—
           Let us part now!

THE FOREST POOL

LEAN down and see your little face
  Reflected in the forest pool,
Tall foxgloves grow about the place,
  Forget-me-nots grow green and cool.
Look deep and see the naiad rise
To meet the sunshine of your eyes.

Lean down and see how you are fair,
  How gold your hair, your mouth how red;
See the leaves dance about your hair
  The wind has left unfilleted.
What naiad of them can compare
With you for good and dear and fair?

THE FOREST POOL

Ah! look no more—the water stirs,
   The naiad weeps your face to see,
Your beauty is more rare than hers,
   And you are more beloved than she.
Fly! fly, before she steals the charms
The pool has trusted to her arms.

DISCRETION

AH, turn your pretty eyes away!
   You would not have me love again?
Love's pleasure does not live a day,
     Immortal is Love's pain,
     And I am tired of pain.

I have loved once—aye, once or twice;
   The pleasure died, the pain lives here;
I will not look in your sweet eyes,
     I will not love you, Dear,
     Lest you should grow too dear.

For I am weary and afraid.
   Have I not seen why life was fair,
And known how good a world God made,
     How sweet the blossoms were,
     How dear the green fields were?

DISCRETION

And I have found how life was gray,
   A mist-hung road, a quest in vain,
Until once more Love smiled my way
     And fooled me once again,
     And taught me grief again.

Now I will gather no more grief;
   I only ask to see the sky,
The budding flower, the budding leaf,
     And put old dreamings by,
     The dreams Love tortures by.

For, being wise, I love no more;
   You, if you will, snare with those eyes
Some fool who never loved before,
     And teach him to be wise!
     For why should you be wise?

SPRING SONG

HERE'S the Spring-time, Sweet!
  Earth's green gown is new,
Lambs begin to bleat,
  Doves begin to coo,
  Birds begin to woo
      In the wood and lane;
Sweet, the tale is true
      Spring is here again!

I have been discreet
  All the winter through;
Now, before your feet,
  Blossoms let me strew.

SPRING SONG

Flowers, as yet, are few;
   Will my lady deign
Take this flower or two?
   Spring is here again

Make the year complete,
   Give the Spring her due!
All the flowers entreat,
   All the song-birds sue.
'Twixt the green and blue
     Let Love wake and reign,
Let me worship you—
     Spring is here again!

TOO LATE

WHEN Love, sweet Love, was tangled in my snare
  I clipped his wings, and dressed his cage with flowers,
  Made him my little joy for little hours,
And fed him when I had a song to spare.
And then I saw how good life's good things were,
  The kingdoms and the glories and the powers.
  Flowers grew in sheaves and stars were shed in showers,
And, when the great things wearied, Love was there.

But when, within his cage, one winter day
  I found him lying still with folded wings,
  No longer fluttering, eager to be fed—
Kingdoms and powers and glories passed away,
  And of life's countless, precious, priceless things
    Nothing was left but Love—and Love was dead!

BY FAITH WITH THANKSGIVING

LOVE is no bird that nests and flies,
No rose that buds and blooms and dies,
No star that shines and disappears,
No fire whose ashes strew the years :
Love is the god who lights the star,
   Makes music of the lark's desire,
Love tells the rose what perfumes are,
   And lights and feeds the deathless fire.

Love is no joy that dies apace
With the delight of dear embrace—
Love is no feast of wine and bread,
Red-vintaged and gold-harvested :

BY FAITH WITH THANKSGIVING

Love is the god whose touch divine
   On hands that clung and lips that kissed,
Has turned life's common bread and wine
   Into the Holy Eucharist.

THE APPEAL

ALL summer-time you said :
"Love has no need of shelter nor of kindness,
For all the flowers take pity on his blindness,
    And lead him to his scented rose-soft bed."

"He is a king," you said.
"That I bow not the knee will never grieve him,
For all the summer-palaces receive him."
    But now Love has not where to lay his head.

"He is a god," you said.
"His altars are wherever roses blossom."
And summer made his altar of her bosom,
    But now the altar is ungarlanded.

THE APPEAL

Take back the words you said :
Out in the rain he shivers broken-hearted ;
Summer who bore him has with tears departed,
    And o'er her grave he weeps uncomforted.

And you, for all you said,
Would weep too, if when dawn stills the wind's riot,
You found him on your threshold, pale and quiet,
    Clasped him at last, and found the child was dead.

AUTUMN SONG

"WILL you not walk the woods with me?
　The shafts of sunlight burn
On many a golden-crested tree
　And many a russet fern.
The Summer's robe is dyed anew,
　And Autumn's veil of mist
Is gemmed with little pearls of dew
　Where first we met and kissed."

"I will not walk the woodlands brown
　Where ghosts and mists are blown,
But I will walk the lonely down
　And I will walk alone.

AUTUMN SONG

Where Night spreads out her mighty wing
   And dead days keep their tryst,
There will I weep the woods of Spring
   Where first we met and kissed."

THE LAST ACT

NEVER a ring or a lock of hair
   Or a letter stained with tears,
No crown for the princely hour to wear,
   To be mocked of the rebel years.
Not a spoken vow, not a written page
   And never a rose or a rhyme
To tell to the wintry ear of age
   The tale of the summer time.

Never a tear or a farewell kiss
   When the time is come to part;
For the kiss would burn and the tear would hiss
   On the smouldering fire in my heart.

THE LAST ACT

But let me creep to the kindly clay,
  And nothing be left to tell
How I played in your play a year and a day,
  And died when the curtain fell!

FAUTE DE MIEUX

WHEN the corn is green and the poppies red
  And the fields are crimson with love-lies-bleeding,
When the elms are black deep overhead
  And the shade lies cool where the calves are feeding,
When the blackbird whistles the song of June,
  When kine knee-deep in the pond are drowsing,
Leave pastoral peace—come up through the noon
  To the high chalk downs where the sheep are browsing.

FAUTE DE MIEUX

Oh! sweet to dream in the noontide heat,
   On the scented bed of thyme and clover,
With the air from the sea, blown keen and sweet,
   And the wings of the wide sky folded over,
While, far in the blue, the skylark sings,
   Renounce desire and renounce endeavour,
Forget life's little unworthy things
   And dream that the dream will last for ever.

The love of your life, in your heart's hid shrine,
   With its gifts and its torments, leave it sighing,
And I will bury the pain of mine
   In the selfsame grave where its joy is lying.
Let me hold your hand for a quiet hour
   In the wild thyme's scent and the clear blue weather,
Then come what may, we have plucked one flower,
   This hour on the downs alone together.

SONG OF LONG AGO

LONG ago, long ago,
When the hawthorn buds were pearly
And the birds sang, late and early,
All the songs that lovers know,
How we lingered in the lane,
Kissed and parted, kissed again,
Parted, laggard foot and slow!
What a pretty world we knew
Dressed in moonlight, dreams and dew,
Long ago, my first sweet sweetheart,
Long ago!

SONG OF LONG AGO

    Long ago, long ago,
When the wind was on the river
Where the lights and shadows shiver,
    And the streets were all aglow.
In the gaudy gas-lit street
We two parted, sweet, my sweet,
    And the crowd went to and fro,
And your veil was wet with tears
For the inevitable years—
    Long ago, my last sweet sweetheart,
               Long ago!

IN ECLIPSE

PALE veil of mist bound round the trees
  Pale fringe of rain upon the hills,
Cold earth, cold sky and biting breeze
  That mock the withered daffodils.
And yet so short a while ago,
  The sunlight on the quickened land
Laughed at the memory of the snow,
  And we went hand in hand.

Pale veil of doubt wound round my heart,
  Pale fringe of tears upon your eyes;
Why did we choose the evil part?
  Why did we leave our Paradise?

IN ECLIPSE

There were such green and pleasant ways
   Where you and I with happy heart
Laughed at the old unhappy days,
   And now—we are apart.

Will the sun shine again some day?
   Will you forgive me and forget?
Chill is the east, the west is gray,
   And all our world with tears is wet.
Ah! love, the world is wide and cold,
   The weary skies are wild with rain;
Give me at least your hand to hold
   Till the sun shines again.

SPECIAL PLEADING

THE world's a path all fresh and sweet,
   A sky all fresh and fair,
With daisies underneath your feet
   And roses for your hair;
Red roses for your pretty hair,
   Green trees to shade your way,
And lavish blossoms everywhere,
   Because the time is May.

How gold the sun shines through the green!
   How soft the turf is spread!
How richly falls the shimmering sheen
   About your darling head!

SPECIAL PLEADING

How in the dawn of Paradise
  Should you foresee the night?
How, with the sunlight in your eyes,
  See aught beyond the light?

*   *   *   *   *

The world's a path all rough and wild,
  A sky all black with fears,
Among the ghosts, unhappy child,
  You stumble, blind with tears;
The track is faint, and far the fold,
  And very far the day:
Unless you have a hand to hold,
  How will you find the way?

"LOVE WELL THE HOUR"

HEART of my heart, my life and light,
   If you were lost what should I do?
I dare not let you from my sight,
   Lest Death should fall in love with you.

Such countless terrors lie in wait.
   The gods know well how dear you are:
What if they left me desolate
   And plucked and set you for their star?

So hold my hand—the gods are strong,
   And perfect joy so rare a flower
No man may hope to keep it long,
   And I might lose it any hour.

"LOVE WELL THE HOUR"

So, kiss me close, my star, my flower,
 Thus shall the future spare me this:
The thought that there was ever an hour
 We might have kissed and did not kiss.

BETRAYED

I WENT back to our home to-day
  That still its robe of roses wore;
My feet took the old easy way,
  And led me to our door.

And you are gone and never more
  Those little feet of yours will come
To meet me at the open door,
  The threshold of our home.

The door unlatched did not protest:
  I entered, and the silence drew
My steps towards the little nest
  That once I shared with you.

BETRAYED

There lay your fan, your open book,
    Your seam half-sewn, and I could see
The window whence you used to look—
    Yes, once you looked—for me.

Print of your little head caressed
    Our pillow still, and on the floor
Still lay, dropped there when last you dressed,
    The scarf and rose you wore.

All should have spoken of you plain,
    Yet, when I bade the silence tell
Of you, my bidding was in vain,
    I could not break its spell.

The silence would not speak, my dear,
    Till the last level light grew dim;
Then, in the twilight I could hear;
    The silence spoke—of him.

THE HEART OF SADNESS

IT is not, Dear, because I am alone,
   For I am lonelier when the rest are near,
But that my place against your heart has grown
   Too dear to dream of when you are not here.

I weep because my thoughts no more may roam
   To meet, half-way, your longing thoughts of me,
To turn with these and spread glad wings for home,
   For the dear haven where I fain would be.

When first we loved, I loved to steal away
   To show to solitude what love could do,
To fill the waste space of the night and day
   With thousand-wingèd dreams that flew to you;

THE HEART OF SADNESS

But now through many tears I am grown wise
   To know how mighty and how dear love is;
I dare not turn to him my longing eyes,
   Nor even in dreams lean out my face to his,

Because, if once I let my caged heart go
   Through dreams to seek you, I should follow too
Through wrong and right, through wisdom and through woe,
   Through heaven and hell, until I won to you!

THE HEART OF JOY

DEAR, do you sigh that your love may not
    stay with you,
        Laugh with and play with you,
        Weep with and pray with you,
          All his life through?
Think, O my heart, if you never had found me,
Crept through the cere-clothes the world has
    wound round me,
        What would you do?

Wide is the world, and so many would sigh for
    you,
        Long for and cry for you,
        Weep for and die for you,
          You being you.

THE HEART OF JOY

I only I, am the man you could sigh for,
Live for and suffer for, sorrow and die for,
      Twenty lives through.

Think! Had I missed you! The world was so wide for us,
      Traps on each side for us,
      Nothing as guide for us,
      Yet I and you
Found Life's great treasure, the last and the first, love;
Life's little things, Time and Space, do their worst, love!
      What, after all, can they do?

THE HEART OF GRIEF

YOU will not come again
Along the deep-banked lane
To where the field and fold so long have missed
you;
You know no more the way
To where, so many a day
Before the world grew gray,
Your lover kissed you.

The wonders and delights
Of London days and nights
Hold fast a soul not made for pastoral pleasures;
The scent of mignonette
Brings to you no regret,
No withered flowers lie yet
Among your treasures.

THE HEART OF GRIEF

    And I, who long for you
    Sad and glad seasons through,
Find my grief's heart in knowing grief will find you;
        Some day you too will sigh,
        And lay a dead flower by,
        And weep to see joy lie
            At last behind you.

    What though the flower you hide
    With London wire be tied?
What though the heart that broke your heart be rotten?
        You too at last must miss
        The smile, the word, the kiss,
        And know how hard it is
            To be forgotten.

REQUIEM

NOW veiled in the inviolable past
   Love lies asleep, who never more will wake;
   Nor would you wake him, even for my sake
Who for your sake pray he sleep sound at last.

What good thing had we of him—we who bore
   So long his yoke? what pleasant thing had we
   That we should weep his deathlong sleep to see,
Or call on Life to waken him once more?

A little joy he gave, and much of pain,
   A little pleasure, and enduring grief,
   One flower of joy, and pain piled sheaf on sheaf,
Harvests of loss, for every bud of gain.

REQUIEM

Yet where he lies in this deserted place
  Divided by his narrow grave we sit,
  Welded together by the depths of it,
Watching the years pass, with averted face.

We do not mourn for him, for here is peace;
  The old unrest frets not these empty years;
  With him went smiles a few, and many tears,
And peace is sweeter far than those or these.

Only—we owe him nothing. If he gave,
  We too gave gifts—his gifts were less than ours:
We gave the world, that held so many flowers
For this—the world that only holds his grave.

TEINT NEUTRE

WIDE downs all gray, with gray of clouds
   roofed over,
   Chill fields stripped naked of their gown of
   grain,
Small fields of rain-wet grass and close-grown
   clover,
   Wet, wind-blown trees—and, over all, the rain.

Does memory lie? For Hope her missal closes
   So far away the may and roses seem;
Ah! was there ever a garden red with roses?
   Ah! were you ever mine save in a dream?

TEINT NEUTRE

So long it is since Spring, the skylark waking
  Heard her own praises in his perfect strain;
Low hang the clouds, the sad year's heart is breaking,
  And mine, my heart—and, over all, the rain.

OUT OF HOPE

IF through the rain and wind along the street,
   Where the wet stone reflects the flickering gas,
Some weeping autumn night your wandering feet,
   Lost in a lonely world, should chance to pass;
If, passing many doors that welcomed you
   When robes of good renown your dear name wore,
Your feet again, as once they used to do,
      Paused at my door,—

Should I shut fast my heart for the old ill,
   The old wrong done, the sorrow and the sin?
Or—only knowing that I love you still—
   Should I throw wide the door and let you in?

OUT OF HOPE

Come—with your sins—my tears shall wash them all,
The heart you broke still waits to be your home.
Yet if you came. . .   Oh! lost beyond recall
You never more will come.

HAUNTED

THE house is haunted; when the little feet
   Go pattering about it in their play,
I tremble lest the little one should meet
   The ghosts that haunt the happy night and day.

And yet I think they only come to me;
   They come through night of ease and pleasant day
To whisper of the torment that must be
   If I some day should be, alas! as they.

And when the child is lying warm asleep,
   The ghosts draw back the curtain of my bed,
And past them through the dreadful dark I creep,
   Clasp close the child, and so am comforted.

HAUNTED

Cling close, cling close, my darling, my delight,
   Sad voices on the wind come thin and wild,
Ghosts of poor mothers crying in the night—
   "Father, have pity—once I had a child!"

A DIRGE

    LET Summer go
To other gardens; here we have no need of her.
She smiles and beckons, but we take no heed
    of her,
  Who love not Summer, but bare boughs and
    snow.

    Set the snow free
To choke the insolent triumph of the year,
With birds that sing as though he still were here,
  And flowers that blow as if he still could see.

A DIRGE

    Let the rose die—
What ailed the rose to blow ? she is not dear to us,
Nor all the summer pageant that draws near to us ;
    Let it be over soon, let it go by !

    Let winter come,
With the wild mourning of the wind-tossed
    boughs
To drown the stillness of the empty house
    To which no more the little feet come home.

IV

EVENING SONG

WHEN all the weary flowers,
Worn out with sunlit hours,
Droop o'er the garden beds
Their little sleepy heads,
The dewy dusk on quiet wings comes stealing;
And, as the night descends,
The shadows troop like friends
To bring them healing.

EVENING SONG

So, weary of the light
Of life too full and bright,
We long for night to fall
To wrap us from it all;
Then death on dewy wings draws near and holds us,
And like a kind friend come
To children far from home,
With love enfolds us.

But when the night is done,
Fresh to the morning sun,
Their little faces yet
With night's sweet dewdrops wet,
The flowers awake to the new day's new graces;
And we, ah! shall we too
Turn to the daydawn new
Our tear-wet faces?

"THIS DESIRABLE MANSION"

THE long white windows blankly stare
    Across the sodden, tangled grass,
Weed-covered are the pathways where
    No footsteps ever pass;
No whispers wake, no kisses die,
    No laughter thrills the dwindling flowers,
Only the night hears sigh on sigh
    From ghosts of long-dead hours.

None come here now to laugh or weep;
    The spider spins on stair and hall,
And round the windows shadows creep,
    And loathly creatures crawl.
Cold is the hearth; the door is fast;
    No guest the silent threshold sees
Save ghosts out of the happy past,—
    And one who is as these.

EBB-TIDE

NOW the vexed clouds, wind-driven, spread wings
 of white,
Long leaning wings across the sea and land.
The waves creep back bequeathing to our sight
 The treasure-house of their deserted sand,
And where the nearer waves curl white and low,
Knee-deep in swirling brine the slow-foot shrimp-
 ers go.

Pale breadth of sand, where clamorous gulls
 confer,
 Marked with broad arrows by their planted
 feet;
White rippled pools, where late deep waters were
 And ever the white waves marshalled in retreat
And the grey wind in sole supremacy
O'er opal and amber cold of darkening sky and
 sea.

ON THE DOWNS

THE little moon is dead,
  Drowned in the flood of rain
That drips from roof of byre and shed,
  And splashes in the lane:
The leafless lean-flanked lane where last year's leaves are spread.

The sheep cower in the fold,
  Where the rain beats them blind,
Where scarce the rotten hurdles hold
  Against the weary wind
That moans with angry tears across the pathless wold.

ON THE DOWNS

Dim lights across the down
  Show where the lone farms lie,
The twisted trees have lost their brown,
  Are black against the sky,
And far below blink lights, gay lights of Brighton town.

Ah, was the moon once bright?
  And did the thyme smell sweet
Where, between dewy dusk and light,
  The warm turf felt our feet,
And bean-flowers scented all the enchanted summer night?

Did sheep-bells tinkle clear
  Across the golden haze?
Were the woods ever leafy-dear,
  In those forgotten days?
The wet wind shrieks denial: no other voice speaks here.

NEW COLLEGE GARDENS, OXFORD

ON this old lawn, where lost hours pass
  Across the shadows dark with dew,
Where autumn on the thick sweet grass
  Has laid a weary leaf or two,
When the young morning, keenly sweet,
  Breathes secrets to the silent air,
Happy is he whose lingering feet
  May wander lonely there.

The enchantment of the dreaming limes,
  The magic of the quiet hours,
Breathe unheard tales of other times
  And other destinies than ours;

NEW COLLEGE GARDENS, OXFORD

The feet that long ago walked here
   Still, noiseless, walk beside our feet,
Poor ghosts, who found this garden dear,
   And found the morning sweet!

Age weeps that it no more may hold
   The heart-ache that youth clasps so close,
Pain finely shaped in pleasure's mould,
   A thorn deep hidden in a rose.
Here is the immortal thorny rose
   That may in no new garden grow—
Its root is in the hearts of those
   Who walked here long ago.

TO A TULIP-BULB

    SLEEP first,
And let the storm and winter do their worst;
Let all the garden lie
Bare to the angry sky,
The shed leaves shiver and die
    Above your bed;
Let the white coverlet
Of sunlit snow be set
    Over your sleeping head,
While in the earth you sleep
Where dreams are dear and deep,
And heed nor wind nor snow,
Nor how the dark moons go.
In this sad upper world where Winter's hand
Has bound with chains of ice the weary land.

TO A TULIP-BULB

    Then wake
To see the whole world lovely for Spring's sake ;
    The garden fresh and fair
    With green things everywhere,
    And winter's want and care
        Banished and fled ;
    Primrose and violet
    In every border set,
        With rain and sunshine fed.
    Then bless the fairy song
    That cradled you so long,
    And bless the fairy kiss
    That wakened you to this—
A world where Winter's dead and Spring doth reign
And lovers whisper in the budding lane.

FEBRUARY

THE trees stand brown against the gray,
  The shivering gray of field and sky;
The mists wrapt round the dying day
  The shroud poor days wear as they die:
Poor day, die soon, who lived in vain,
Who could not bring my Love again!

Down in the garden breezes cold
  Dead rustling stalks blow chill between;
Only, above the sodden mould,
  The wallflower wears his heartless green
As though still reigned the rose-crowned year
And summer and my Love were here.

FEBRUARY

The mists creep close about the house,
　The empty house, all still and chill ;
The desolate and trembling boughs
　Scratch at the dripping window sill :
Poor day lies drowned in floods of rain,
And ghosts knock at the window pane.

THE PROMISE OF SPRING

JUST a whisper, half-heard,
But our heart knows the word;
Caresses that seem
Like love's lips in a dream;
 Yet we know she is here,
 The desirèd, the dear,
 The love of the year!
 In the murmur of boughs,
 In the softening of skies,
 In the sun on the house,
 In the daffodil's green
 (Half an inch, half-unseen

THE PROMISE OF SPRING

Mid the mournful brown mould
Where the rotten leaf lies)
Her story is told.

O Spring, darling Spring,
O sweet days of blue weather!
The thrushes shall sing,
Fields shall grow green again,
Daisies be seen again,
Hedges grow white;
Then down the lane,
Grown leafy again,
Shall go lovers together—
Lovers who see again
    Sunshine and showers,
    Perfume and flowers,
    Dewy dear hours,
        Dream and delight.

THE PROMISE OF SPRING

Warm shall nests be again,
Winter's behind us;
Springtime shall find us,
Taking our hands,
Lead us away from the cold and the snow,
Into the green world where primroses grow.
Winter, hard winter, forgotten, forgiven;
All the old pain paid, to seventy times seven,
    All the new glory a-glow.
Love, when Spring calls, will you still turn
    away?
Winter has wooed you in vain, and shall
    May?
        Love, when Spring calls, will you
        go?

MEDWAY SONG

(*Air: Carnaval de Venise*)

LET Housman sing of Severn shore,
   Of Thames let Arnold sing,
But we will sing no river more
   Save this where crowbars ring.
Let others sing of Henley,
   Of fashion and renown,
But we will sing the thirteen locks
   That lead to Tonbridge town!
Then sing the Kentish river,
   The Kentish fields and flowers,
We waste no dreams on other streams
   Who call the Medway ours.

MEDWAY SONG

When on the level golden meads
    The evening sunshine lies,
The little voles among the reeds
    Look out with wondering eyes.
The patient anglers linger
    The placid stream beside,
Where still with towering tarry prow
    The stately barges glide.
Then sing the Kentish river,
    The Kentish fields and flowers,
We waste no dreams on other streams
    Who call the Medway ours.

On Medway banks the May droops white,
    The wild rose blossoms fair,
O'er meadow-sweet and loosestrife bright,
    For water nymphs to wear.
And mid the blowing rushes
    Pan pipes a joyous song,

MEDWAY SONG

And woodland things peep from the shade
    As soft we glide along.
Then sing the Kentish river,
    The Kentish fields and flowers,
We waste no dreams on other streams
    Who call the Medway ours.

You see no freight on Medway boats
    Of fashions fine and rare,
But happy men in shabby coats,
    And girls with wind-kissed hair.
The world's a pain forgotten,
    And very far away,
The stream that flows, the boat that goes—
    These are our world to-day.
Then sing the Kentish river,
    The Kentish fields and flowers,
We waste no dreams on other streams
    Who call the Medway ours.

CHAINS INVISIBLE

THE lilies in my garden grow,
  Wide meadows ring my garden round,
In that green copse wild violets blow,
  And pale, frail cuckoo flowers are found.
For all you see and all you hear,
  The city might be miles away,
And yet you feel the city near
  Through all the quiet of the day.

Sweet smells the earth—wet with sweet rain—
  Sweet lilac waves in moonlight pale,
And from the wood beyond the lane
  I hear the hidden nightingale.

CHAINS INVISIBLE

Though field and wood about me lie,
  Hushed soft in dew and deep delight,
Yet can I hear the city's sigh
  Through all the silence of the night.

For me the skylark builds and sings,
  For me the vine her garland weaves;
The swallow folds her glossy wings
  To build beneath my cottage eaves.
But I can feel the giant near,
  Can hear his slaves by daylight weep,
And, when at last the night is here,
  I hear him moaning in his sleep.

Oh! for a little space of ground,
  Though not a flower should make it gay,
Where miles of meadows wrapped me round,
  And leagues and leagues of silence lay.

CHAINS INVISIBLE

Oh! for a wind-lashed, treeless down,
  A black night and a rising sea,
And never a thought of London town,
  To steal the world's delight from me.

AT EVENING TIME THERE SHALL BE LIGHT

THE day was wild with wind and rain,
    One grey wrapped sky and sea and shore,
It seemed our marsh would never again
    Wear the rich robes that once it wore.
The scattered farms looked sad and chill,
    Their sheltering trees writhed all awry,
And waves of mist broke on the hill
    Where once the great sea thundered by.

Then God remembered this His land,
    This little land that is our own,
He caught the rain up in His hand,
    He hid the winds behind His throne,
He soothed the fretful waves to rest,
    He called the clouds to come away,
And, by blue pathways, to the west,
    They went, like children tired of play.

AT EVENING TIME

And then God bade our marsh put on
    Its holy vestment of fine gold ;
From marge to marge the glory shone
    On lichened farm and fence and fold ;
In the gold sky that walled the west,
    In each transfigured stone and tree,
The glory of God was manifest,
    Plain for a little child to see !

MAIDENHOOD

THROUGH her fair world of blossoms fresh
    and bright,
Veiled with her maiden innocence, she goes;
Not all the splendour of the waxing light
    She sees, nor all the colour of the rose;
And yet who knows what finer hues she sees,
    Hid by our wisdom from our longing eyes?
Who knows what light she sees in skies and seas
    Which is withholden from our seas and skies?

Shod with her youth the thorny paths she treads
    And feels not yet the treachery of the thorn,
Her crown of lilies still its perfume sheds
    Where Love, the thorny crown, not yet is borne.
Yet in the mystery of her peaceful way
    Who knows what fears beset her innocence,
Who, trembling, learns that thorns will wound
    some day,
    And wonders what thorns are, and why, and
    whence?

V

THE MONK

WHEN in my narrow cell I lie,
   The long day's penance done at last,
I see the ghosts of days gone by,
   And hear the voices of the past.

I see the blue-gray wood-smoke curled
   From hearths where life has rhymed to love,
I see the kingdoms of the world—
   The glory and the power thereof,

THE MONK

And cry, " Ah, vainly have I striven ! "
    And then a voice calls, soft and low :
" Thou gavest My Earth to win My Heaven ;
    But Heaven-on-Earth thou mayest not know ! "

It is not for Thy Heaven, O Lord,
    That I renounced Thy pleasant earth—
The ship, the furrow, and the sword—
    The dreams of death, the dreams of birth !

Weary of vigil, fast, and prayer,
    Weak in my hope and in my faith—
O Christ, for whom this cross I bear,
    Meet me beside the gate of Death !

When the night comes, then let me rest
    (O Christ, who sanctifiest pain !)
Falling asleep upon Thy breast,
    And, if Thou wilt, wake never again !

THE CROWN OF LIFE

THE days, the doubts, the dreams of pain
Are over, not to come again,
And from the menace of the night
Has dawned the day-star of delight:
My baby lies against me pressed—
Thus, Mother of God, are mothers blessed!

His little head upon my arm,
His little body soft and warm,
His little feet that cannot stand
Held in the heart of this, my hand.
His little mouth close on my breast—
Thus, Mary's Son, are mothers blessed.

THE CROWN OF LIFE

All dreams of deeds, all deeds of day
Are very faint and far away,
Yet you some day will stand upright
And fight God's foes, in manhood's might,
You—tiny, worshipped, clasped, caressed—
Thus, Mother of God, are mothers blessed.

Whatever grief may come to be
This hour divine goes on for me.
All glorious is my little span,
Since I, like God, have made a man,
A little image of God's best—
Thus, Mary's Son, are mothers blessed.

Come change, come loss, come worlds of tears,
Come endless chain of empty years;
They cannot take away the hour
That gives me You—my bird, my flower!
Thank God for this! Leave God the rest!—
Thus, Mother of God, are mothers blessed.

MAGNIFICAT

THIS is Christ's birthday: long ago
   He lay upon His Mother's knee,
Who kissed and blessed Him soft and low—
   God's gift to her, as you to me.

My baby dear, my little one,
   The love that rocks this cradling breast
Is such as Mary gave her Son:
   She was more honoured, not more blest.

He smiled as you smile: not more sweet
   Than your eyes were those eyes of His,
And just such little hands and feet
   As yours Our Lady used to kiss.

MAGNIFICAT

The world's desire that Mother bore:
   She held a King upon her knee:
O King of all my world, and more
   Than all the world's desire to me!

I thank God on the Christmas morn,
   For He has given me all things good:
This body which a child has borne,
   This breast, made holy for his food.

High in high heaven Our Lady's throne
   Beside her Son's stands up apart:
I sit on heaven's steps alone
   And hold my king against my heart.

Across dark depths she hears your cry;
   She sees your smile, through worlds of blue
Who was a mother, even as I,
   And loved her Child, as I love you.

MAGNIFICAT

And to her heart my babe is dear,
    Because she bore the Babe Divine,
And all my soul to hers draws near,
    And loves Him for the sake of mine!

EVENING PRAYER

NOT to the terrible God, avenging, bright,
  Whose altars struck their roots in flame and blood,
Not to the jealous God, whose merciless might
  The infamy of unclean years withstood ;
But to the God who lit the evening star,
  Who taught the flower to blossom in delight,
Who taught His world what love and worship are
            We pray, we two, to-night.

EVENING PRAYER

To no vast Presence too immense to love,
   To no enthronèd King too great to care,
To no strange Spirit human needs above
   We bring our little, intimate, heart-warm
     prayer;
But to the God who is a Father too,
   The Father who loved and gave His only Son
We pray across the cradle, I and you,
        For ours, our little one!

CHRISTMAS HYMN

O CHRIST, born on the holy day,
    I have no gift to give my King;
No flowers grow by my weary way;
    I have no birthday song to sing.

How can I sing Thy name and praise,
    Who never saw Thy face divine;
Who walk in darkness all my days,
    And see no Eastern stars a-shine?

Yet, when their Christmas gifts they bring,
    How can I leave Thy praise unsung?
How stay from homage to the King,
    And hold a silent, grudging tongue?

CHRISTMAS HYMN

Lord, I found many a song to sing,
    And many a humble hymn of praise
For Thy great Miracle of Spring,
    The wonder of the waxing days.

When I beheld Thy days and years,
    Did I not sing Thy pleasant earth?
The moons of love, the years of tears,
    The mysteries of death and birth?

Have I not sung with all my soul
    While soul and song were mine to yield,
Thy lightning crown, Thy cloud-control,
    The dewy clover of Thy field?

Have I not loved Thy birds and beasts,
    Thy streams and woods, Thy sun and shade;
Have I not made me holy feasts
    Of all the beauty Thou hast made?

CHRISTMAS HYMN

What though my tear-tired eyes, alas!
   Won never grace Thy face to see?
I heard Thy footstep on the grass,
   Thy voice in every wind-blown tree.

No music now I make or win,
   Yet, Lord, remember I have been
The lover of Thy world, wherein
   I found nought common or unclean.

Grown old and blind, I sing no more,
   Thy saints in heaven sing sweet and strong,
Yet take the songs I made of yore
   For echoes to Thy birthday song.

ABSOLUTION

UNBIND thine eyes, with thine own soul confer,
  Look on the sins that made thy life unclean,
Behold how poor thy vaunted virtues were,
    How weak thy faith, thy deeds how small and mean,
    How far from thy high dreams thy life hath been,
  How poor thy use of all thou hast received,
How little of all God's glory thou hast seen,
    How misconstrued that which thou hast perceived.

Turn not thine eyes away from thine unworth,
  The cup of shame drink to the bitter lees;

ABSOLUTION

And when thou art lowerèd to the least on earth,
  And in the dust makest common cause with these,
  Then shall kind arms enfold thee, bringing peace,
    The Earth, thy Mother, shall assuage thy pain,
  Her woods and fields, Her quiet streams and seas
    Shall touch thy soul, and make thee whole again.

But if thy heart holds fast one secret sin,
  If one vile script thy soul shrinks to erase,
The mighty Mother cannot bring thee in
  Unto the happy, holy, healing place;
  But thou shalt weep in darkness, out of grace,
    And miss the light of beauty undefiled;
  For he who would behold Her, face to face,
    Must be in spirit as a little child.

www.ingramcontent.com/pod-product-compliance
Lightning Source LLC
Chambersburg PA
CBHW020254170426
43202CB00008B/372